The Disciples Conclusion Workbook

Dr. Aaron R. Jones

The Disciples Conclusion WORKBOOK

Copyright © 2015 by Dr. Aaron R. Jones

Printed in the Unites States of America

Published by Kingdom Kaught Publishing, LLC, Denton, Maryland

All rights reserved. No part of this book may be reproduced or transmitted in any form or by any means, electronic or mechanical, including photocopying, recording or by any information storage and retrieval system without written permission from the author, except for the inclusion of brief quotations in a review.

All scripture quotations are from the King James Version of the Bible. Thomas Nelson Publishers, Nashville: Thomas Nelson, Inc. 1972.

Editor: Sharon D. Jones

Copy editing: Antonio M. Palmer

ISBN: 978-0-9961267-1-7

Table of Contents

CONCLUSION 1
Must make Jesus the #1 priority 1

CONCLUSION 2
Must stay on the path 7

CONCLUSION 3
Must count the price (cost) 11

CONCLUSION 4
Must not cling to earthly possessions 15

CONCLUSION 5
Must be productive 19

6 CONCLUSION
Must have passion 23

7 CONCLUSION
Must know his position 27

8 CONCLUSION
Must be willing to press 31

9 CONCLUSION
Must be prepared to forgive 35

10 CONCLUSION
Must be one of prayer 39

11 CONCLUSION
Must have positive obedience 43

12 CONCLUSION
Must have a purged heart 47

13 CONCLUSION
Must fulfill the Great Commission 51

INTRODUCTION

I want to introduce what I believe is a vital concept that will assist every disciple in their relationship with the Lord. This workbook has been created to be an aid in what I call the 3 "A" Principle to Discipleship. I believe every disciple must ask the tough questions about their walk with Jesus. I believe as we apply this principle, it will be a tool to please the Father.

Let us briefly look at the components of this principle:

Step #1—Admit

Admitting that we fall short of God's standards can be very challenging, but it must be done. Admitting means self-examination of one's walk as a disciple of Jesus Christ. A part of admitting is having a discussion between you and God. Admitting will allow you to see what God sees and see the things that have been ignored.

Step #2—Align

Identify scriptures that state, support, or enhance your position on discipleship. These scriptures should be the catalyst to help you align yourself with Jesus' purpose of a disciple. This is where you want to find yourself in the Word of God. In this step you are seeking revelation from God.

Step #3—Application

Application is the most vital part of the 3 "A" Principle. It allows you to apply the admitting and the aligning. Application is where you make the steps to living out the true disciple's life.

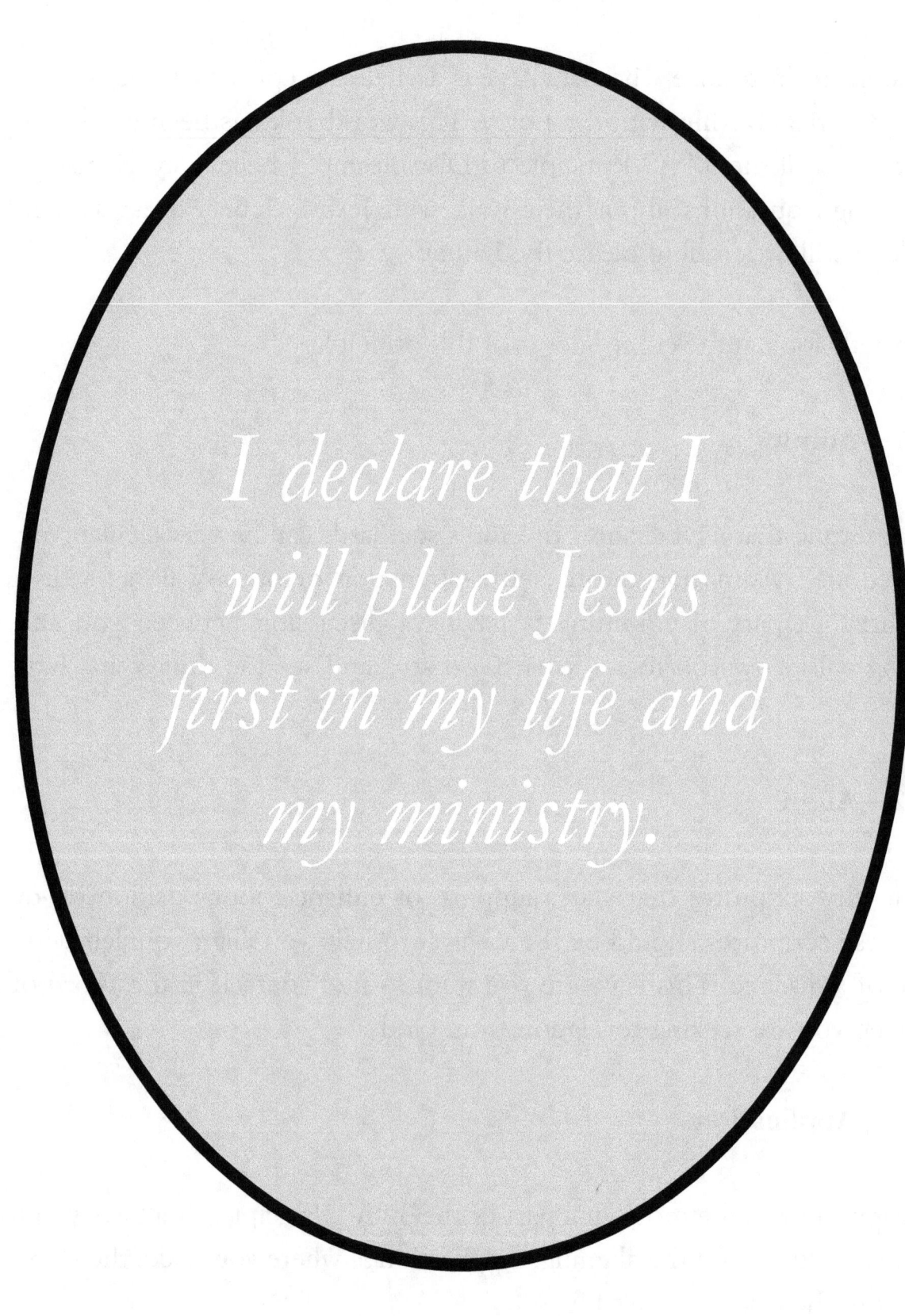

I declare that I will place Jesus first in my life and my ministry.

CONCLUSION 1

Jesus Must be the #1 Priority

"If any man come to me, and hate not his father, and mother, and wife, and children, and brethren, and sisters, yea, and his own life also, he cannot be my disciple." —Luke 14:26

Step #1—Admit

> *At times, our basic needs become a hindrance because we have placed the flesh as our priority.*

What have I placed before Jesus?

1. _____
2. _____
3. _____
4. _____
5. _____

What has taken my attention away from my kingdom assignment?

1. _____
2. _____
3. _____
4. _____
5. _____

What must I add in and subtract from my life so that Jesus can remain as a #1 priority?

1._____
2._____
3._____
4._____
5._____

Step #2—Align

"But seek ye first the kingdom of God, and his righteousness; and all these things shall be added unto you."—Matthew 6:33

> *We must follow after the Spirit to keep Jesus first. When we follow after the Spirit, the flesh is not a priority.*

| Identify 3 more scriptures that reference Jesus as #1 in our lives. |

1._____

2._____

3._____

What special revelation from God have you received?
_____
_____

Step #3—Application

What will I do differently to place Christ first in my life?

1. _____
2. _____
3. _____

The Disciples Conclusion Workbook

[*This page is intentionally left blank*]

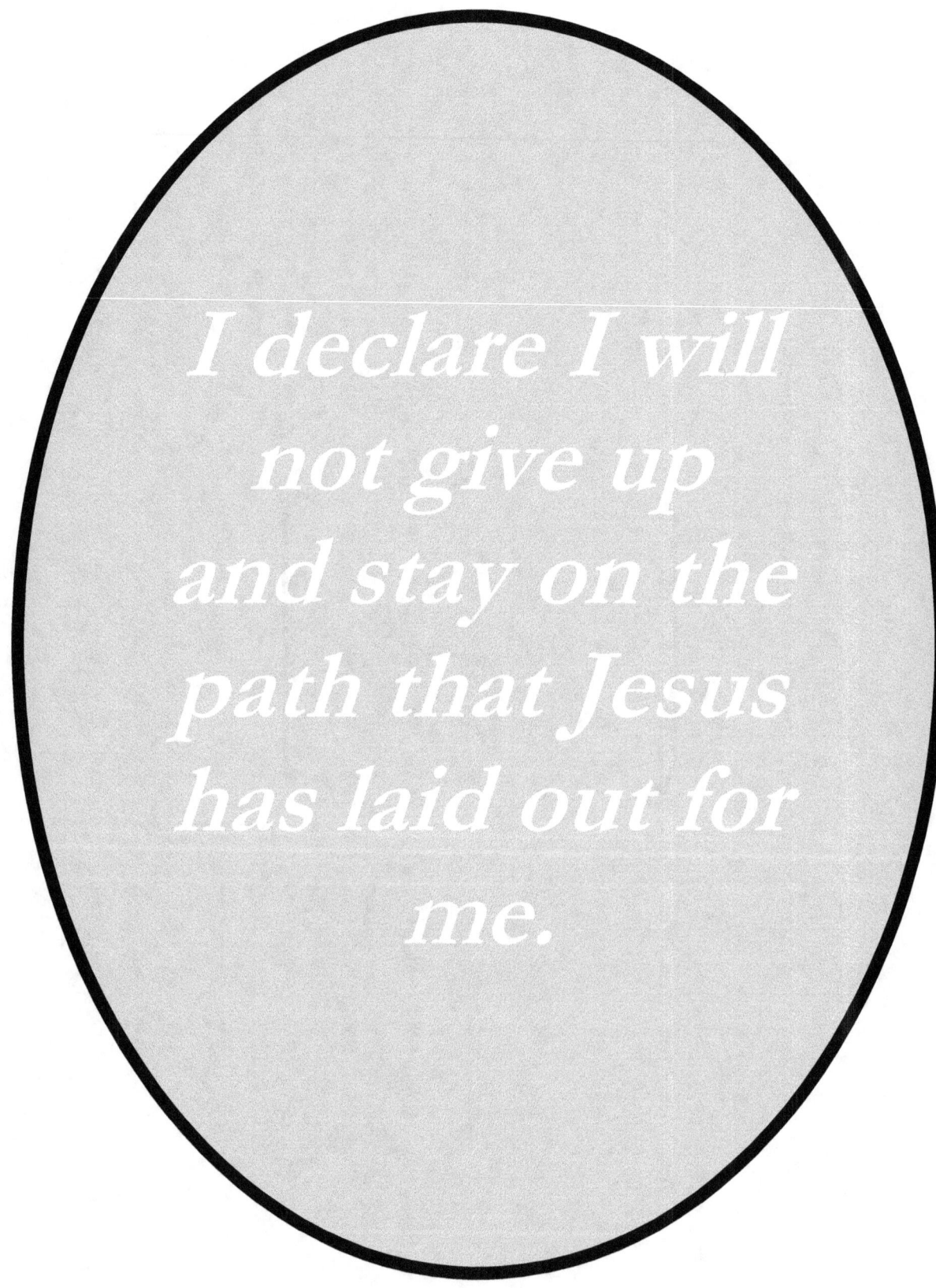

I declare I will not give up and stay on the path that Jesus has laid out for me.

CONCLUSION 2

Must Stay on the Path (Journey)

"And whosoever doth not bear his cross, and come after me cannot be my disciple."
– Luke 14:27

Step#1—Admit

> *Many people do not realize that we can do all the right things and still follow the wrong path.*

Do I have a "stop following Jesus" clause?

_____
_____
_____

Are my decisions controlling my path in a negative way?

_____
_____
_____

What is my response to the enemy when turbulent times arise?

_____
_____
_____

Step #2—Align

[*Disciples cannot afford to lose focus while entertaining the distractions of Satan.*]

"Jesus saith unto him, I am the way, the truth, and the life: no man cometh unto the Father, but by me." – John 14:6

> Identify 3 more scriptures that will keep you on the path of Jesus.

1. _____

2. _____

3. _____

What special revelation from God have you received?
_____
_____

Step #3—Application

1. _____
2. _____
3. _____

The Disciples Conclusion Workbook

The Disciples Conclusion Workbook

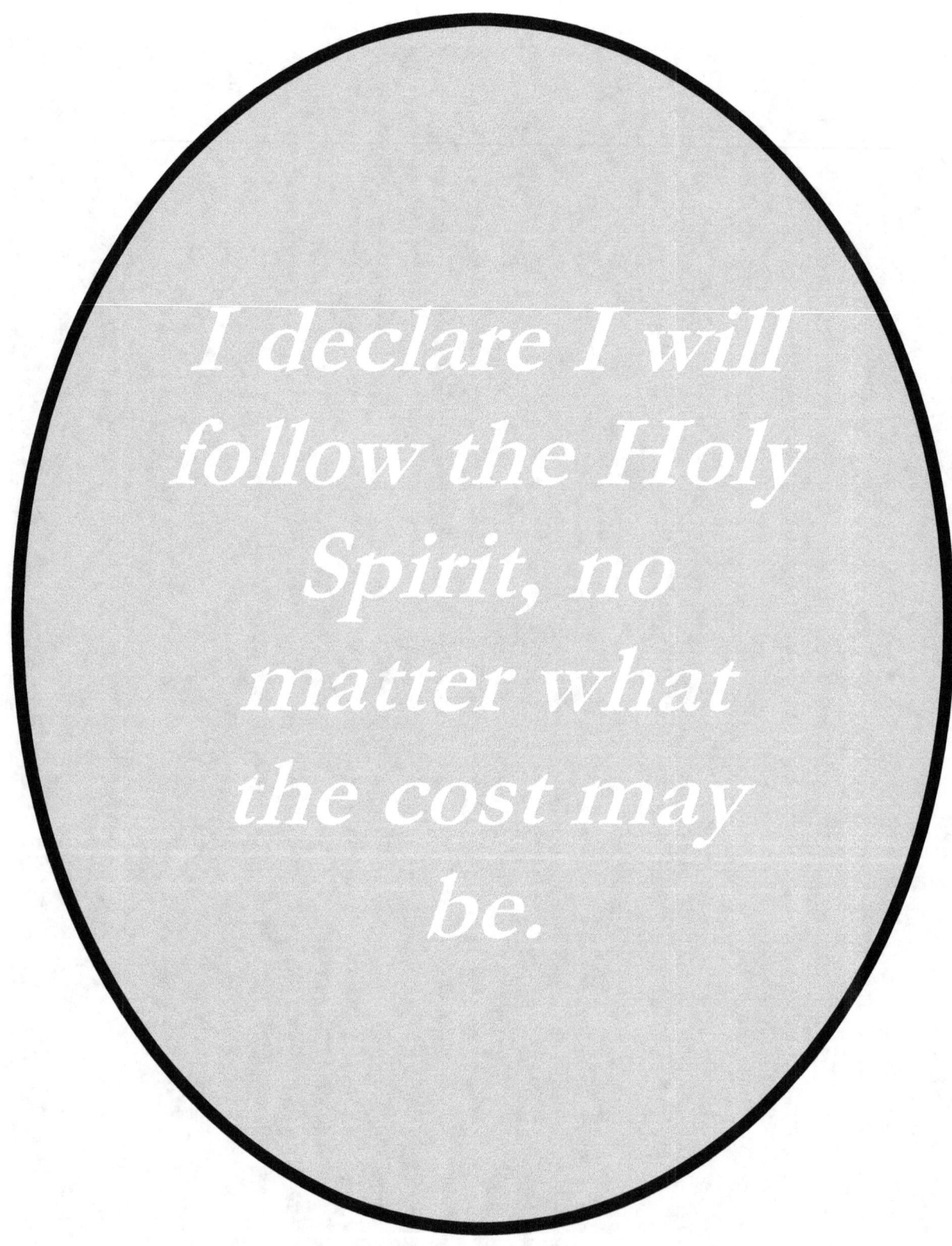

I declare I will follow the Holy Spirit, no matter what the cost may be.

CONCLUSION

Must Count the Price (Cost)

"For which of you, intending to build a tower, sitteth not down first, and counteth the cost, whether he have sufficient to finish it? – Luke 14:28

Step #1—Admit

What cost have you counted since you came to the Lord?

> *God wants the disciple to make counting the cost a part of his daily lifestyle.*

_____
_____
_____

Does your worship cost you anything?

_____
_____
_____

What will you lose? Are you ready to lose it for the Kingdom?

_____
_____
_____

Step #2—Align

"For I reckon that the sufferings of this present time are not worthy to be compared with the glory which shall be revealed in us."—Romans 8:18

> *In view of eternity, following Jesus will cost a disciple something and it is always worth it.*

Identify 3 more scriptures that will you help count the cost.

1. _____

2. _____

3. _____

What special revelation from God have you received?
_____
_____

Step #3—Application

1. _____
2. _____
3. _____

The Disciples Conclusion Workbook

> *I declare I will not allow my material possessions to control my relationship with Jesus.*

CONCLUSION 4

Must Not Cling to Earthly Possessions

"So likewise, whosoever he be of you that forsaketh not all that he hath, he cannot by my disciple"
– Luke 14:33

Step #1—Admit

What possessions in your life have a bigger hold on you than Jesus Christ?

> *There is a mindset, "The more possessions one has, the more power and influence he has."*

1. _____
2. _____
3. _____
4. _____
5. _____

What possessions do you want? Now compare it to what you need.

1. _____
2. _____
3. _____
4. _____
5. _____

Can you release your possessions in order to fulfill God's greater plan?

_____
_____
_____

Step #2—Align

"Lay not up for yourselves treasures upon earth, where moth and rust doth corrupt, and where thieves break through and steal."—Matthew 6:19

{ *The strong desire to have material things hinder one's effectiveness in the Kingdom.* }

| Identify 3 more scriptures that will help me not cling to material possessions. |

1. _____

2. _____

3. _____

What special revelation from God have you received?

_____
_____

Step #3—Application

1. _____
2. _____
3. _____

I declare I will strive to be productive for the Kingdom of God and bear much fruit.

CONCLUSION 5

A Disciple Must Be Productive

"Herein is my Father glorified, that ye bear much fruit; so shall ye be my disciples." – John 15:8

Step #1--Admit

What do I need to do to abide more in Jesus?

> *Reproduction should be in the mind of every disciple. The role of every disciple is to make disciples.*

1. _____
2. _____
3. _____
4. _____
5. _____

Have I lost my saltiness?

_____
_____
_____

Step #2—Align

"I am the vine, ye are the branches: He that abideth in me, and I in him, the same bringeth forth much fruit: for without me ye can do nothing."—John 15:5

> *The disciple is a branch, and God expects every productive branch to bear fruit.*

> Identify 3 more scriptures that will help you be more productive for the kingdom.

1. _____

2. _____

3. _____

What special revelation from God have you received?
_____
_____

Step #3—Application

What must I do to be more productive for Jesus?

1. _____
2. _____
3. _____

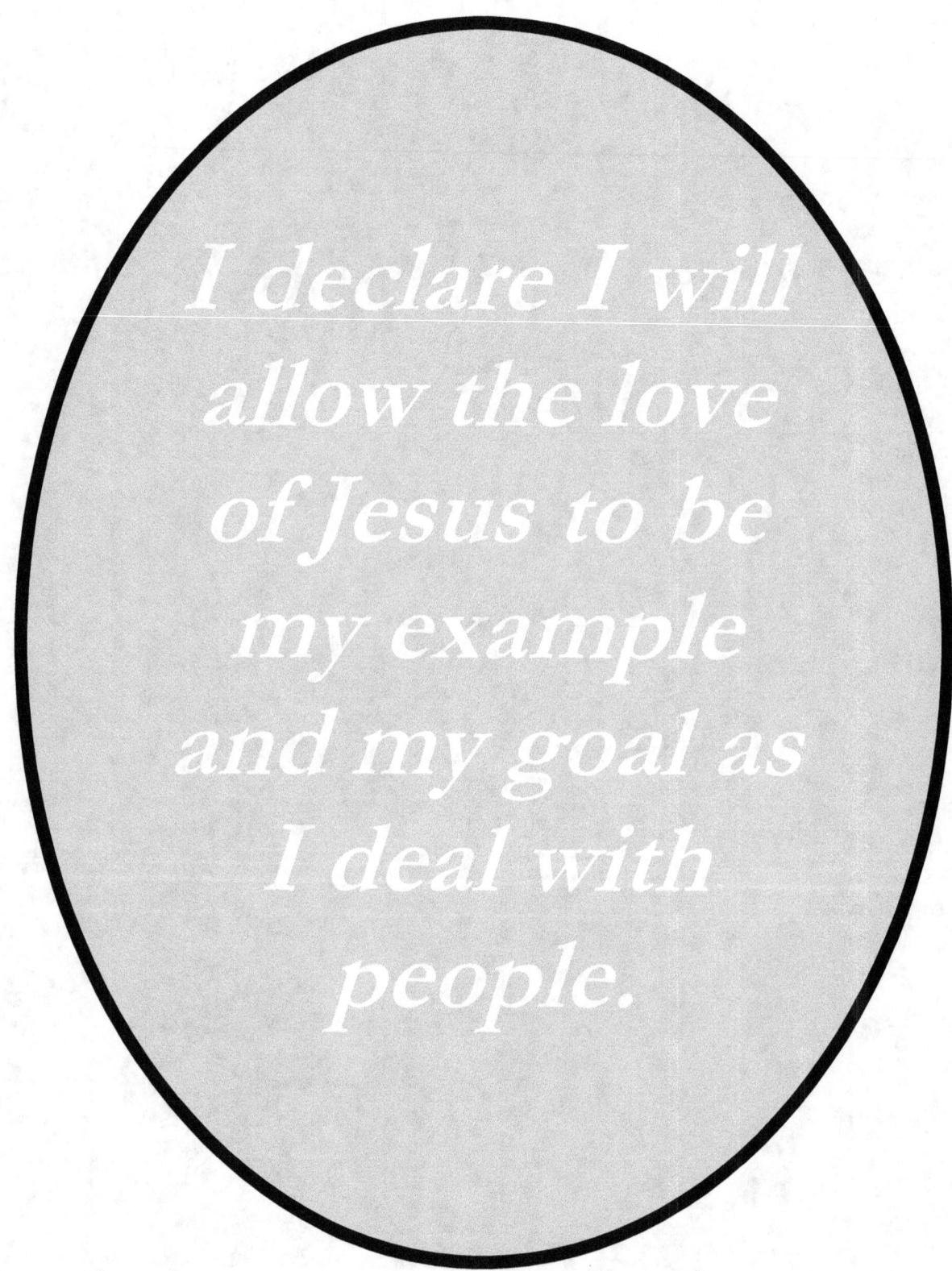

I declare I will allow the love of Jesus to be my example and my goal as I deal with people.

CONCLUSION

Must Have Passion

"By this shall all men know that ye are my disciple, if ye have love one to another."
– John 13:35

Step #1—Admit

Who have you placed on the un-love list of your life because of unforgiveness?
Do they have a relationship with Jesus?

> *We cannot separate love from our lives or Christian walk, because it is the defining point that describes our relationship with Jesus Christ.*

1. _____
2. _____
3. _____
4. _____
5. _____

Do I always practice unconditional love?

_____
_____
_____

Is my love tank empty?

_____
_____
_____

Step #2—Align

"For God so loved the world, that he gave his only begotten Son, that whosoever believeth in him should not perish, but have everlasting life."—John 3:16

> *Love is not an option, but a commandment from God.*

| Identify 3 more scriptures that will help you love like Jesus. |

1. _____
2. _____
3. _____

What special revelation from God have you received?

_____
_____

Step #3—Application

1. _____
2. _____
3. _____

I declare I will always be in the position of a servant and allow my Master, Jesus Christ to reign in my life.

CONCLUSION

Must know his position

"The disciple is not above his master, nor the servant above his lord." —Matthew 10:24

Step #1—Admit

What areas of your life are you still trying to be the Master?

> *The role as a disciple is a servant, and Jesus is the Master. There should never be any confusion about these two roles.*

1. _____
2. _____
3. _____
4. _____
5. _____

What is your role as a servant to Jesus Christ?

1. _____
2. _____
3. _____
4. _____
5. _____

Have you stepped into the Master's lane today?

_____
_____
_____

Step #2—Align

"His lord said unto him, 'Well done, good and faithful servant; thou hast been faithful over a few things, I will make thee ruler over many things: enter thou into the joy of thy lord.'"
—Matthew 25:23

> *A disciple must understand he doesn't have enough wisdom or control to be the Master.*

| Identify 3 more scriptures that will help you be more productive for the kingdom. |

1. _____

2. _____

3. _____

What special revelation from God have you received?
_____
_____

Step #3—Application

1. _____
2. _____
3. _____

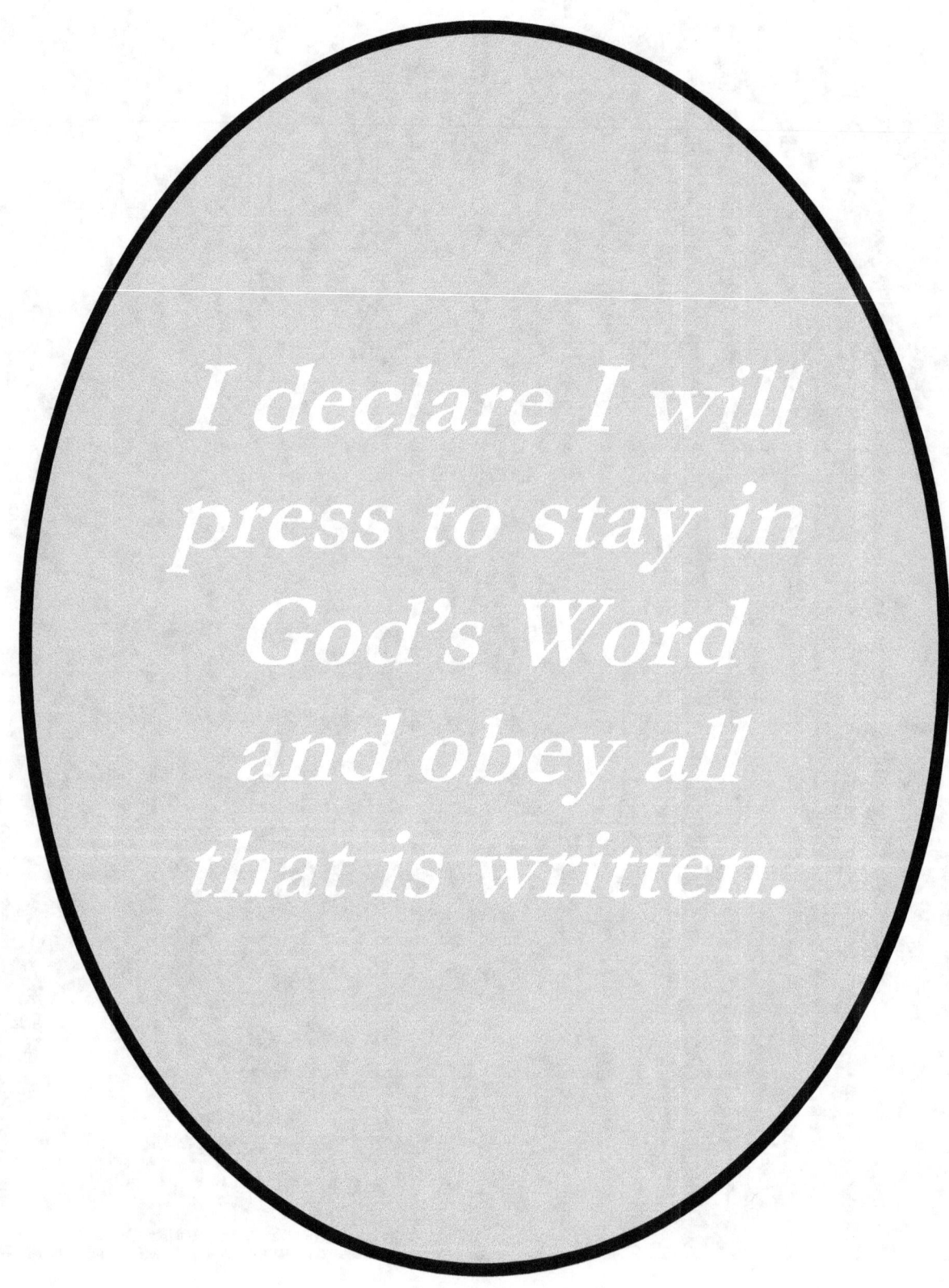

I declare I will press to stay in God's Word and obey all that is written.

CONCLUSION

Must be willing to Press

"Then said Jesus to those Jews which believed on Him, "If ye continue in my word, then are ye my disciples indeed."—John 8:31

Step #1—Admit

> *In order for a disciple to remain the person God has called him to be, he must press into the Word of God.*

Have you lost the hunger for God's Word?

_____
_____
_____

Does the Word of God truly guide your life?

_____
_____
_____

Step #2—Align

"All scripture is given by inspiration of God, and is profitable for doctrine, for reproof, for correction, for instruction in righteousness: That the man of God may be perfect, thoroughly furnished unto all good works."—2 Timothy 3:16, 17.

> *For disciples, the Word of God is our rulebook for Christian living.*

Identify 3 more scriptures that will help you to press in God's Word.

1. _____

2. _____

3. _____

What special revelation from God have you received?
_____
_____

Step #3—Application

What must you do to increase your time in the Word of God?

1. _____
2. _____
3. _____

I declare I will forgive my neighbor of all of his offences toward me.

CONCLUSION

Must be Prepared to forgive

"For if ye forgive men their trespasses, your heavenly Father will also forgive you:"
—Matthew 6:14

Step #1—Admit

> *I consider unforgiveness as unneeded luggage that we carry around.*

Do you have any unforgiveness in your heart?

_____
_____
_____

Do you have limits to your forgiveness?

_____
_____
_____

Are you selective when it comes to forgiveness?

_____
_____
_____

Step #2—Align

"Therefore if thou bring thy gift to the altar, and there rememberest that thy brother hath ought against thee; Leave there thy gift before the altar, and go thy way; first be reconciled to thy brother, and then come and offer thy gift."—Matthew 5:23, 24

> *A disciple must forgive if he wants forgiveness, and to have his sacrifice received by God.*

Identify 3 more scriptures that will help you to forgive like Jesus.

1. _____

2. _____

3. _____

What special revelation from God have you received?
_____
_____

Step #3—Application

1. _____
2. _____
3. _____

The Disciples Conclusion Workbook

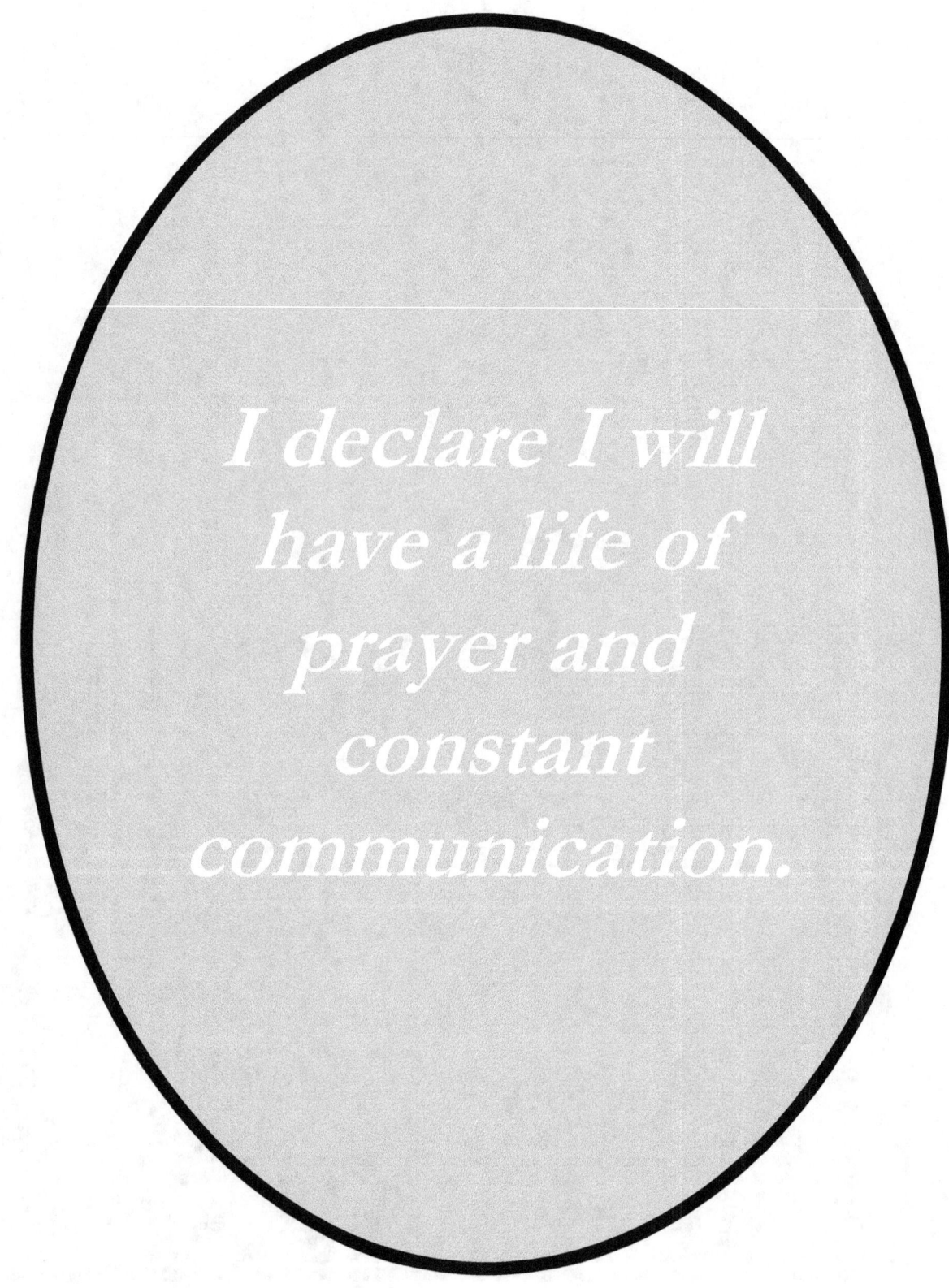

I declare I will have a life of prayer and constant communication.

CONCLUSION

Must be one of Prayer

"And he spake a parable unto them to this end, that men ought always to pray, and not to faint."
— Luke 18:1

Step #1—Admit

> *A disciple does not only pray, but also has a lifestyle of prayer.*

Do you have a consistent prayer life?

_____
_____
_____

Do you go to God only when you need Him?

_____
_____
_____

Do you truly trust God when you pray?

_____
_____
_____

Step #2—Align

"Continue in prayer, and watch in the same with thanksgiving."—Colossians 4:2

The Disciples Conclusion Workbook

> *Prayer should not be a last resort; it is the disciple's only resort.*

Identify 3 more scriptures that address the importance of prayer.

1. _____

2. _____

3. _____

What special revelation from God have you received?
_____
_____

Step #3—Application

1. _____
2. _____
3. _____

I declare I will respond in positive obedience and be intentional about hearing the Voice of God.

CONCLUSION

Must have positive obedience

"If ye love me, keep my commandments." – John 14:15

Step #1—Admit

> *Obedience will challenge every area of the disciple's life. If there isn't obedience; there isn't a relationship.*

Have you substituted sacrifices for obedience?

1. _____
2. _____
3. _____
4. _____
5. _____

Are you determined to obey all of God's Word?

_____
_____
_____

Where are you lacking in obedience to the Lord?

_____
_____
_____

Step #2—Align

"And Samuel said, 'Hath the LORD as great delight in burnt offerings and sacrifices, as in obeying the voice of the LORD? Behold, to obey is better than sacrifice, and to hearken than the fat of rams.'" —1 Samuel 15:22

> *Running from what God is telling us to do is blatant disobedience.*

Identify 3 more scriptures that will help you be more obedient.

1. _____

2. _____

3. _____

What special revelation from God have you received?
_____
_____

Step #3—Application

1. _____
2. _____
3. _____

I declare I will allow God to daily purge my heart.

12
CONCLUSION

Must have a purged heart

"Create in me a clean heart, O God; and renew a right spirit within me." – Psalm 51:10

Step #1—Admit

> One's heart determines what type of disciple he will become.

Do you have spiritual heart troubles?

_____
_____
_____

Is your heart growing closer to Jesus daily?

_____
_____
_____

Do you have a purged heart?

_____
_____
_____

Step #2—Align

> The heart speaks and identifies who we are in relation to the Kingdom.

"O generation of vipers, how can ye, being evil, speak good things? for out of the abundance of the heart the mouth speaketh."
—Matthew 12:34

The Disciples Conclusion Workbook

> Identify 3 more scriptures that will help purge your heart.

1. _____

2. _____

3. _____

What special revelation from God have you received?
_____
_____

Step #3—Application

1. _____
2. _____
3. _____

The Disciples Conclusion Workbook

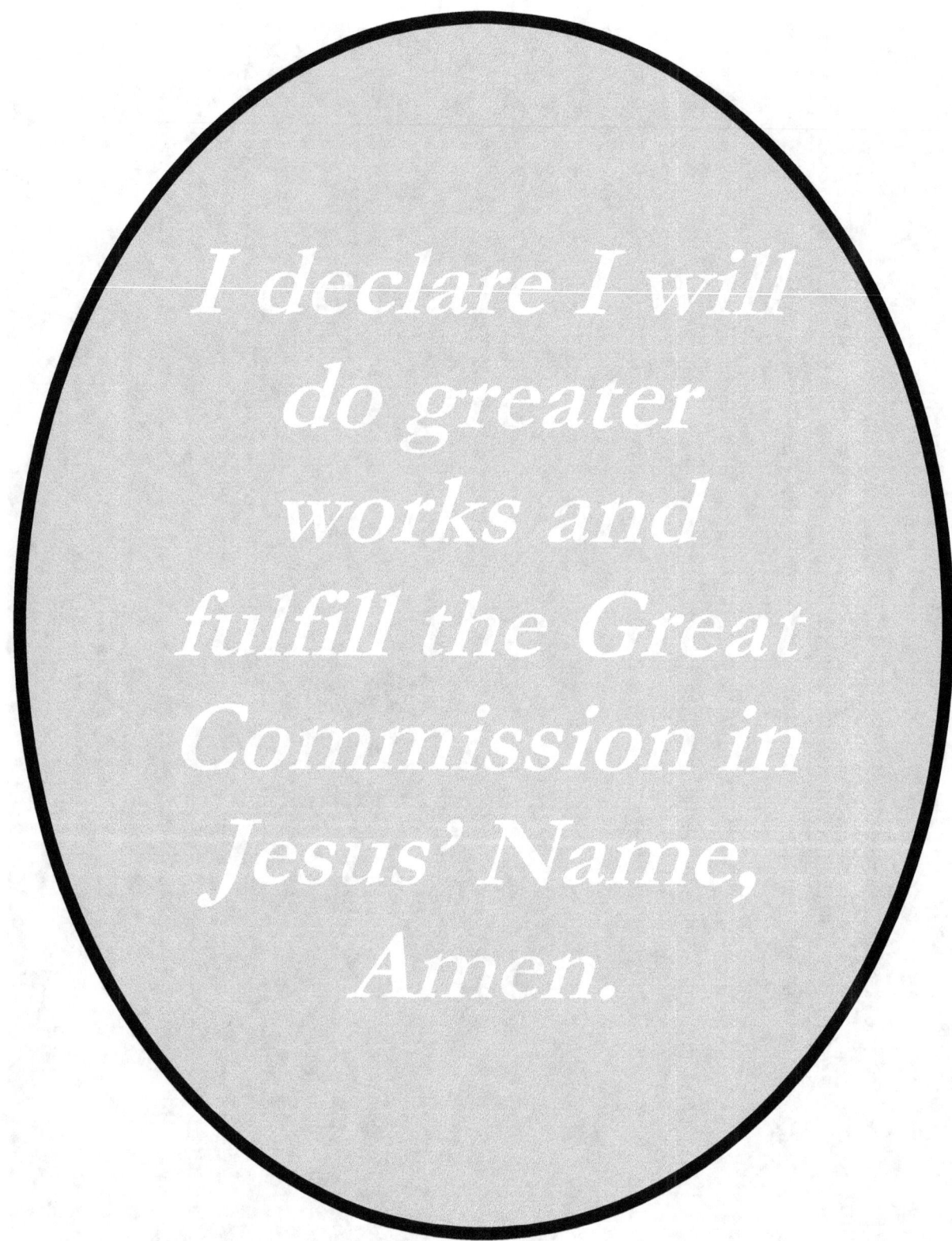

I declare I will do greater works and fulfill the Great Commission in Jesus' Name, Amen.

CONCLUSION

Must fulfill the Great Commission

And Jesus came and spake unto them, saying, "All power is given unto me in heaven and in earth. Go ye therefore, and teach all nations, baptizing them in the name of the Father, and of the Son, and of the Holy Ghost: Teaching them to observe all things whatsoever I have commanded you: and, lo, I am with you always, even unto the end of the world. Amen."
– Matthew 28:18:18-20

Step #1—Admit

> It has been said that the Great Commission is the only commission.

What will you do with the words of Jesus?

_____
_____
_____

Is the Great Commission your personal mission?

_____
_____
_____

Have you witnessed the gospel of Jesus Christ to someone today (this week; this month; this year)?

_____
_____
_____

Step #2—Align

> The greatest work a disciple can do is to help someone come to the saving knowledge of Jesus Christ.

"But ye shall receive power, after that the Holy Ghost is come upon you: and ye shall be witnesses unto me both in Jerusalem, and in all Judaea, and in Samaria, and unto the uttermost part of the earth."—Acts 1:8

Identify 3 more scriptures that express your role to fulfill the Great Commission.

1. _____

2. _____

3. _____

What special revelation from God have you received?
_____
_____

Step #3—Application

1. _____
2. _____
3. _____

www.ingramcontent.com/pod-product-compliance
Lightning Source LLC
Chambersburg PA
CBHW082247300426
44110CB00039B/2470